P9-CQX-653

# Birds

**Susan Canizares** • **Pamela Chanko**

Scholastic Inc.
New York • Toronto • London • Auckland • Sydney

**Acknowledgments**

**Science Consultants:** Patrick R. Thomas, Ph.D., Bronx Zoo/Wildlife Conservation Park;
Glenn Phillips, The New York Botanical Garden
**Literacy Specialist:** Ada Cordova, District 2, New York City

**Design**: MKR Design, Inc.

**Photo Research:** Barbara Scott

**Endnotes**: Samantha Berger

**Endnote Illustrations**: Craig Spearing

---

Photographs: Cover: M.C. Chamberlain/DRK Photo; p. 1: Wayne Lankinen/DRK Photo; p. 2: James
R. Fisher/DRK Photo; p. 3: Michael Fogden/DRK Photo; p. 4: John Cancalosi/DRK Photo;
p. 4b: Schafer & Hill/Peter Arnold; p. 5: Staffan Widstrand/The Wildlife Collection; p. 6: David
Middleton/NHPA; p. 6b: Anthony Mercieca/Photo Researchers, Inc.; p.7: Joe McDonald/DRK Photo;
p. 8: Marc Epstein /DRK Photo; p. 9: M.C. Chamberlain/DRK Photo; p. 10: Wayne Lynch/DRK Photo;
p. 10b: Margot Conte/Animals, Animals; p. 11: Martin Harvey/The Wildlife Collection; p.12: Stephen J.
Krasemann/DRK Photo.

No part of this publication may be reproduced in whole or in part, or stored in a retrieval system, or transmitted
in any form or by any means, electronic, mechanical, photocopying, recording, or otherwise, without
written permission of the publisher. For information regarding permission, write to
Scholastic Inc., 555 Broadway, New York, NY 10012.

Library of Congress Cataloging-in-Publication Data
Canizares, Susan
Birds / Susan Canizares, Pamela Chanko.
p. cm. -- (Science emergent readers)
Includes index.
Summary: Indicates that although various kinds of birds differ
greatly in appearance, all of them have common features including
feathers, beaks, and tails.
ISBN 0-590-76966-9 (pbk.: alk. paper)
1. Birds--Anatomy--Juvenile literature. [1. Birds.]
I. Pamela Chanko, 1968-. II. Title III. Series.
QL676.C26    1998

598--dc21                                                                                  98-18820
                                                                                           CIP AC

Copyright © 1998 by Scholastic Inc.
Illustrations copyright © 1998 by Scholastic Inc.
All rights reserved. Published by Scholastic Inc.
Printed in the U.S.A.

11   12   13   14   15   16   17   18   19   20        08        03   02

What do all birds have?

All birds have wings.

All birds have feathers.

All birds have bills.

All birds have tails.

All birds have feet.

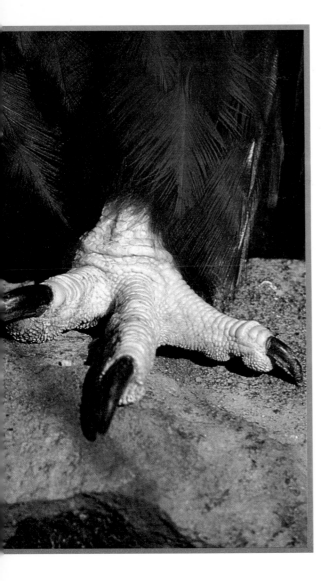

And all birds come from eggs.

# Birds

Birds come in many different shapes and sizes. But no matter how different they look, there are some things they all have in common.

Many male birds look different during the breeding season. The male goldfinch (page 1) is bright while mating in spring, but in winter he turns a bland brown color and looks like a completely different bird!

Whether they fly or not, all birds have wings. The screech owl (pages 2–3) almost quadruples in size when its wings are extended! The owl uses its wings to fly and to quietly swoop down to capture its prey.

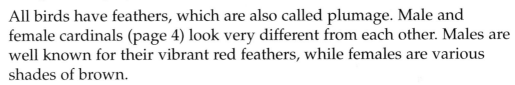

All birds have feathers, which are also called plumage. Male and female cardinals (page 4) look very different from each other. Males are well known for their vibrant red feathers, while females are various shades of brown.

The hoatzin (pages 4–5), of South America, has unique feathers. The young hoatzin actually has claws on its feathers, which help it to climb and grasp limbs. Adult hoatzins lose these claws, but use their wings to help them climb.

The orange-winged parrot (page 5) is actually mostly green with only a patch of orange secondary feathers. It occasionally fluffs and ruffles its feathers, which creates air pockets that help it store heat and stay warm. It's similar to the way people wear layers of clothing to keep warm.

Beaks also come in many different shapes and sizes. Bald eagles (page 6) use their beaks to tear into their prey, mostly fish.

The saddle billed stork (pages 6–7) depends strongly on the shape and coordination of its beak to feed. It either wades in the water and stabs at the fish it sees or sweeps its bill randomly through the water and catches fish when it makes contact!

The male indigo bunting (page 7) has a very small, precise beak. This beak is especially well suited for helping it to get the small seeds and insects it lives on.

Tails vary from bird to bird as well, and some birds show them more than others! The northern pintail (page 8) can often be found tail-side-up. It feeds mostly by night, going completely upside down to reach for roots and tubers.

The male peacock (pages 8–9) is most well known for its huge feather display, which many think is its tail. But the long and colorful fan is not actually its tail, but is made up of 150 large feathers that grow from its lower back! The real tail is short, dull colored, and hidden underneath the train!

Birds have many different kinds of feet too. The red footed booby (page 10) has webbed feet, which are especially good for swimming.

The condor (pages 10–11) has extremely sharp claws, called talons, which it uses when hunting its prey. The condor can sweep down, curl its talons around its victim, and lift it into the air.

The yellow-crowned night heron (page 11) has legs especially well suited for its behavior and environment. Its long thin legs make it less visible when wading in water to catch fish. It can also use its legs for gripping sticks and roots.

When all birds begin life, they hatch from eggs. This emperor goose (page 12) is waiting for her eggs to hatch. This goose breeds in the Arctic tundra in a nest hollow lined with moss, grass, and down. How many goslings do you think might hatch?